If there were no **bad people**, there would be no **good lawyers**.

Charles Dickens

Charles Dickens

Born: Portsmouth, England, 1812

Died: Kent, England, 1870

Mostly self-educated, and always hardworking,
Dickens' literary success followed employment
in a boot polish factory, the humiliation of
seeing his father in a debtor's prison, and
clerking in a solicitor's office. He established
himself as a reporter and short story writer at
the age of 17, and fame came in 1836 with the
first installment of *The Pickwick Papers*. His
14 completed novels have never been out of
print, most famously, *A Christmas Carol* and
Great Expectations.

NOËL COWARD

I like LONG WALKS, especially when they are taken by PEOPLE who ANNOY me.

Noël Coward

Born: London, England, 1899
Died: Jamaica, West Indies, 1973

A consummate actor, raconteur, director, playwright, entertainer, songwriter, and painter, Coward, known as "The Master," made his theater debut at age 12, and for the next six decades was never out of the limelight. He wrote some 37 plays, including *Private Lives* and *Blithe Spirit*, 300 songs, 16 musicals, and appeared in many films. His portrayal of Mr. Bridger, a crime boss pulling the strings from prison in *The Italian Job*, has become legend.

Tact is the ART of making a POINT without making an ENEMY.

Isaac Newton

Isaac Newton

Born: near Grantham, Lincolnshire, England, 1642
Died: London, England, 1727

One of the greatest scientific minds of all
time, Newton's contributions include optics,
three laws of motion, the universal law of
gravitation, calculus, and the principles of
modern physics. While a student, and later
as Lucasian Professor of Mathematics at
Cambridge University (1661–1696), an apple
falling from a tree in Trinity College
gardens prompted his study of gravity.
Newton was knighted in 1705 and is buried
in Westminster Abbey in London.

I find that the **HARDER I WORK,** the **MORE LUCK** I seem to **HAVE.**

Thomas Jefferson

Thomas Jefferson

Born: Shadwell, Virginia, 1743
Died: Monticello, Virginia, 1826

One of the Founding Fathers, Jefferson inspired the "new America" with his ideals of political and religious freedom, and education reforms. Decades before he became the country's third president (1801–1809), Jefferson drafted the Declaration of Independence, including the famous phrase: "all men are created equal." Despite his strongly held principles, Jefferson also "owned" 600 slaves and instituted the forceful removal of Native Peoples from their land.

Let us all be HAPPY, and live WITHIN our MEANS, even if we have to BORROW the MONEY to do it with.

CHARLES FARRAR BROWNE

Charles Farrar Browne

Born: Waterford, Maine, 1834

Died: Southampton, England, 1867

The career of this humorist started when he wrote letters from a fictitious and unsophisticated showman, Artemus Ward, to magazines like *Vanity Fair* and later *Punch*. His letters, sketches, and travel stories were full of misspellings and misused words, all played for comic effect. Browne, as Ward, went on the lecture circuit, his shows attracting huge audiences in the US and UK, and he is considered the US's first stand-up comedian.

Oscar Wilde

Born: Dublin, Ireland, 1854
Died: Paris, France, 1900

The son of a surgeon and a writer, Wilde gained celebrity for his poetry, novels and plays, as well as his private life. Among his best-known works are *The Picture of Dorian Gray* and *The Importance of Being Earnest*. His final work, *The Ballad of Reading Gaol*, told of Wilde's two-year prison sentence with hard labor. On his release in 1897, he fled to Paris where he died, aged 46, alone and destitute. He was buried in Père Lachaise, Paris.

Better a Witty Fool than a Foolish Wit.

William Shakespeare

William Shakespeare

Born: Stratford-upon-Avon, England, 1564
Died: Stratford-upon-Avon, England, 1616

The Bard of Avon—regarded as the greatest dramatist of all time, his work has been translated into 80 languages—became an actor, playwright, and part owner of a theatrical company in his twenties. By 1592, his work was sufficiently known for him to be called an "upstart Crow" by a critic. From 1589 to 1613, he wrote 39 plays and 154 sonnets. He divided his time between Stratford, where his family lived, and London and his Globe Theatre.

Mae West

Born: New York City, New York, 1893
Died: Hollywood, California, 1980

West was hitting the boards in
vaudeville from age five, and by
1928 she was the talk of Broadway,
and in demand in Hollywood.
Famous for her risqué double
entendres and open sensuality,
West was the first woman to write
the films in which she starred. The
characters she usually played had
progressive or questionable morals
and sharp, witty voices.

Rudyard Kipling

Born: Mumbai, India, 1865

Died: Middlesex Hospital, London, 1936

After enduring several miserable years in England for his schooling, Kipling returned to his Indian "paradise" to become a journalist. Success with his story collections encouraged him to travel. *The Jungle Book* and his poem "If–" were written in the US in 1892 and 1895. By 1907, he had not only won over readers around the world but also the judges of the Nobel Prize for Literature. Kipling's books for children have never been out of print.

Always do right; this will gratify some people and astonish the rest.

Mark Twain

Mark Twain

Born: Florida, Missouri, 1835
Died: Redding, Connecticut, 1910

Samuel Langhorne Clemens' family moved to Hannibal, on the Mississippi River, when he was just four. The river later inspired his *The Adventures of Huckleberry Finn*, but it was when he was working as a newspaper printer that he discovered his love and talent for writing. Clemens' time as a riverboat pilot resulted in his famous pen name—Mark Twain. A "mark twain" indicated that the depth of the water was two fathoms and safe for navigation.

If we do what is necessary, all the odds are in our favor.

Charles Buxton

Charles Buxton

Born: Norfolk, England, 1822
Died: Loch Earn, Scotland, 1871

Charles Buxton followed in his father's
footsteps, joining the family's brewing
business and being a member of
parliament, liberal philanthropist, and noted
supporter of the abolition movement. A
modest but prosperous man, he enjoyed
thinking, and he recorded his thoughts and
observations of events and nature in his
journals. A collection of Buxton's journals,
Notes of Thought, was published in 1883 and
remains a culturally significant document.

Take care of the luxuries and the necessities will take care of themselves.

DOROTHY PARKER

Dorothy Parker

Born: Long Branch, New Jersey, 1893
Died: New York City, New York, 1967

Born Dorothy Rothschild, Parker described
herself as "a plain disagreeable child... with
a yen to write poetry." After *Vanity Fair*
published one of her poems, she joined
Vogue and later became its drama critic.
Her writing was known for its wit—a
misjudged quip got her fired from *Vogue*—
and cynicism. She was a literary celebrity of
1920s New York, but found writing hard
work and once commented that for every
five words she wrote, she changed seven!

Elbert Hubbard

Born: Bloomington, Illinois, 1856

Died: at sea, off Ireland, 1915

A writer and publisher, Hubbard produced
monthly brochures and magazines through
his Roycroft Press (inspired by William
Morris' arts and crafts Kelmscott Press) on
famous people and events. His writing
blended fact with comment and satire, and
his belief in the value of working with "head,
hand, and heart" led to a Roycroft studio for
artists and craftspeople. Hubbard and his
wife were on board the RMS *Lusitania* when
it was sunk by a German torpedo.

ADVICE is Seldom WELCOME, and those who need it MOST, like it LEAST.

Philip Stanhope,
4th Earl of Chesterfield

Philip Stanhope

Born: London, England, 1694
Died: London, England, 1773

The 4th Earl of Chesterfield, this canny, tactical politician and diplomat was known for the wit of his speeches, the power of his debating, and his philosophy on life. Stanhope's philosophy is exemplified in *Letters to His Son on the Art of Becoming a Man of the World and a Gentleman*. This volume consists of 30 years of advice-loaded correspondence from Stanhope to his son Philip.

DOGS are BETTER than human beings because they KNOW but do not TELL.

Emily Dickinson

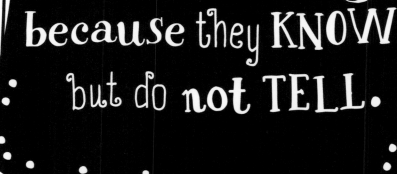

Emily Dickinson

Born: Amherst, Massachusetts, 1830
Died: Amherst, Massachusetts, 1886

One of the US's most beloved and original poets, Dickinson often wrote of immortality and death. While at college, she refused to declare her faith in religion, preferring to keep faith in science. Dickinson lived a simple, reclusive life in the same house all her life, and was thought of as an eccentric. Of her 1,800 poems, only a handful, including "Hope is the thing with feathers…" and "I'm Nobody! Who are you?" were published in her lifetime.

It's not the

years in your

LIFE

that count.

It's the

LIFE

in your years.

Abraham Lincoln

Abraham Lincoln

Born: Hodgenville, Kentucky, 1809
Died: Washington, D.C., 1865

The US's 16th president may be best known for his emancipation legislation, which opened the way for the abolition of slavery. A towering figure of the American Civil War (1861–1865) and author of the Gettysburg Address, Lincoln was born in a log cabin and self-educated. He taught himself law and won his first state election in 1834. Shot by John Wilkes Booth at Ford's Theatre, he was the first US president to be assassinated.

Choose A Job

You

LOVE,

»and«

you will never

HAVE to WORK

a day in your

LIFE.

« CONFUCIUS »

Confucius

Born: Lu (Shandong Province), China, 551 BCE
Died: Lu (Shandong Province), China, 479 BCE

Almost 2,500 years have passed since Confucius' death, but his philosophy still resonates throughout Asia and beyond. Born to a poor rural family, Confucius was self-taught, formulating his ethical principles while working as a clerk for a local landowner. For many years, his teachings about doing right and being selfless fell on the deaf ears of China's feuding princes, but flowered among the country's oppressed millions.

Groucho Marx

Born: New York City, New York, 1890
Died: Los Angeles, California, 1977

Julius Henry Marx and his four brothers
performed in vaudeville when they were
young, initially as a singing troupe, then later,
more successfully, as comedians. Nicknamed
for his moodiness, Groucho's greasepaint
eyebrows and moustache, spectacles, and
stooped walk were all for show – only the cigar
and fast talking were real. The Marx Brothers'
26 films included *Horse Feathers* and *A Day at
the Opera*. Groucho's suggestion for his
gravestone was: "Excuse me, I can't stand up."

I have great faith in fools;

self-confidence my friends call it.

Edgar Allan Poe

Edgar Allan Poe

Born: Boston, Massachusetts, 1809
Died: Baltimore, Maryland, 1849

Poe's body of work includes poetry, short stories, a novel, and countless reviews and features. He is widely acknowledged as an early master of science fiction, Gothic horror, and whodunit detective mysteries. It was *The Raven*, published in 1845, that established his reputation and allowed him to live by writing alone—an American first! Poe's other standout works include *The Pit and the Pendulum*, *The Fall of the House of Usher*, and *Murders in the Rue Morgue*.

I HAVE NOT FAILED.
I'VE JUST FOUND
10,000 WAYS
THAT WON'T WORK.

THOMAS EDISON

Thomas Edison

Born: Milan, Ohio, 1847

Died: West Orange, New Jersey, 1931

Edison held a world-record 1,093 patents, testament to the man and the team he established at the world's first research laboratory—Menlo Park in New Jersey. His first invention was the tinfoil phonograph. This was soon followed by the incandescent light bulb. The "Wizard of Menlo Park," as he was known, developed a motion picture camera, the Kinetograph, a starter battery for Henry Ford's Model T, and more.

Behold the TURTLE. HE makes PROGRESS only WHen he STICKS his NECK OUT.

James BryaNT CoNaNT

James Bryant Conant

Born: Dorchester, Massachusetts, 1893
Died: Hanover, New Hampshire, 1978

This noted research chemist was
instrumental in the development of the
atomic bomb, and after World War Two was
the US consul in West Germany. As
president of Harvard University, Conant was
committed to education reform. Motivated
by egalitarian principles, he abolished
mandatory Latin classes and athletic
scholarships, introduced coeducational
classes and made it possible for women to
attend Harvard medical and law schools.

Honesty pays, but it don't seem to pay **ENOUGH** to suit some people.

Kin Hubbard

Kin Hubbard

Born: Bellefontaine, Ohio, 1868

Died: Indianapolis, Indiana, 1930

The youngest of five siblings, Frank
McKinney Hubbard did not excel at school—
he was always sketching. He worked as a
newspaper artist, but without formal training
his drawings remained "crude." This style
though, suited Hubbard's cartoon, *Abe
Martin of Brown County,* that ran in
newspapers for an incredible 26 years! The
characters of Brown County became
Hubbard's spokespeople for his down-to-
earth quips and political and social humor.

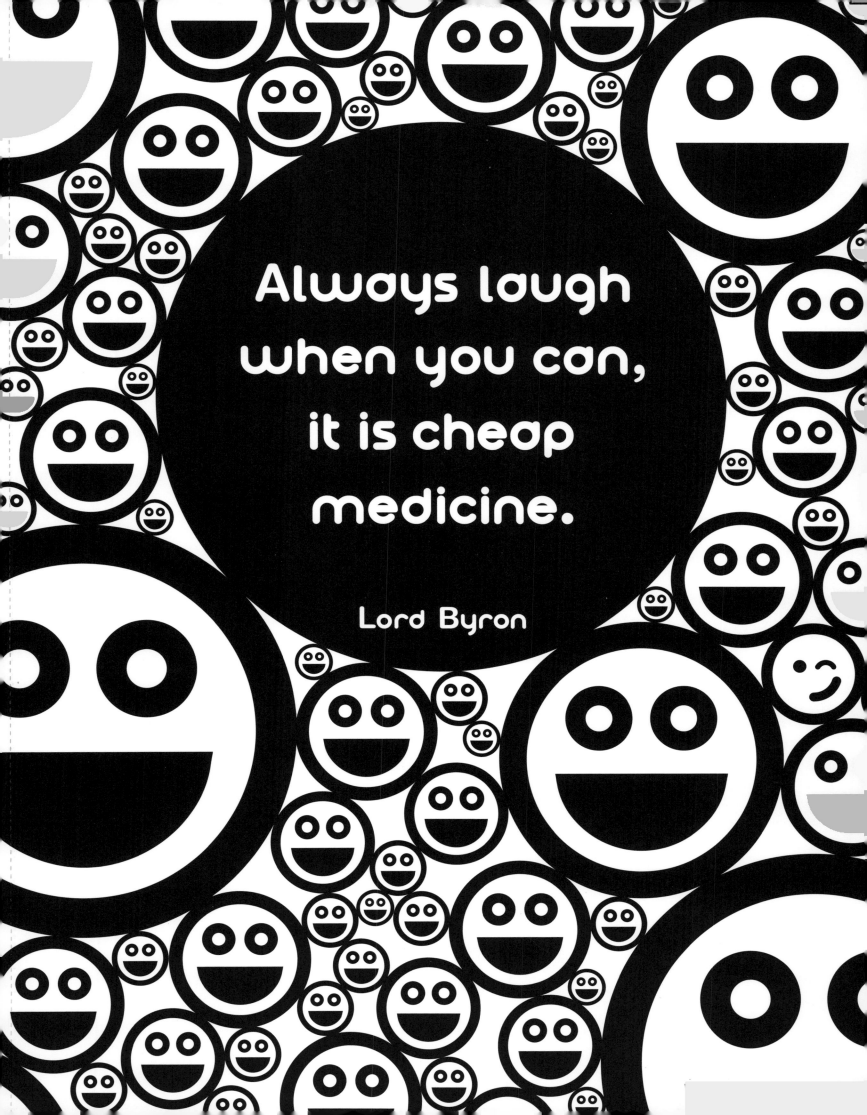

Always laugh when you can, it is cheap medicine.

Lord Byron

Lord Byron

Born: London, England, 1788
Died: Missolonghi, Greece, 1824

Byron inherited his title and estate at age 10, but neither compensated for his insecurity about his clubfoot. Early poems tell of his sadness when a girl cast him aside as "that lame boy." She may have regretted doing so when *Childe Harold's Pilgrimage* was published in 1812, making Byron a celebrity. Such was his reputation for excess, scandal, and openness to experiences, the phrase "mad, bad and dangerous to know" was penned specifically about him.

A LIFE spent making mistakes is NOT ONLY MORE honorable, BUT MORE useful than a LiFE SPENT DOiNG NOTHiNG.

GEORGE BERNARD SHAW

George Bernard Shaw

Born: Dublin, Ireland, 1856

Died: Ayot St. Lawrence, England, 1950

On moving to London in 1876, Shaw worked
as a critic before defining himself as a
dramatist. His play *Arms and the Man* (1894)
established his reputation for stylistically
unconventional and politically radical and
witty—often caustic—commentaries on
society and religion. In all he wrote 60 plays,
including *Pygmalion*, *Saint Joan*, and *Man
and Superman*, and in 1925, he was awarded
the Nobel Prize for Literature, confirming his
profound influence on theater.